First published in 2005 by Grolier
An imprint of Scholastic Library Publishing
Old Sherman Turnpike
Danbury, Connecticut 06816

© 2005 Graham Beehag Books

For information address the publisher:
Scholastic Library Publishing, Old Sherman Turnpike,
Danbury, Connecticut 06816

Library of Congress Cataloging-in-Publication Data

Arnold, James R.
    The industrial revolution / James R. Arnold and Roberta Wiener.
      p. cm
    Includes bibliographical references and index.
    Contents: v. 1. A turning point in history – v. 2. The industrial revolution begins – v. 3. The industrial revolution spreads – v. 4. The industrial revolution comes to America – v. 5. The growth of the industrial revolution in America – v. 6. The industrial revolution spreads through Europe – v. 7. The worldwide industrial revolution – v. 8. America's second industrial revolution – v. 9. The industrial revolution and the working class v. 10. The industrial revolution and American society.
    ISBN 0-7172-6031-3 (set)—ISBN 0-7172-6032-1 (v. 1)—
    ISBN 0-7172-6033-X (v. 2)—ISBN 0-7172-6034-8 (v. 3)—
    ISBN 0-7172-6035-6 (v. 4)—ISBN 0-7172-6036-4 (v. 5)—
    ISBN 0-7172-6037-2 (v. 6)—ISBN 0-7172-6038-0 (v. 7)—
    ISBN 0-7172-6039-9 (v. 8)—ISBN 0-7172-6040-2 (v. 9)—
    ISBN 0-7172-6041-0 (v. 10)
    1. Industrial revolution. 2. Economic history. I. Wiener, Roberta.
II. Title.

HD2321.A73 2005
330.9'034–dc22   2004054243

Printed and bound in China

CONTENTS

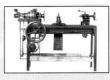

THE REVOLUTION IN MACHINE TOOLS

The revolutionary changes in the pacesetting industries that began the Industrial Revolution—textiles, iron, and mining—gave dramatic proof that a new era had begun. Those changes could not have occurred without simultaneous advances in a more fundamental sector, the machine tool industry. James Watt's steam engine, for instance, had needed metal cylinders accurately fabricated so that a piston fit precisely throughout the length of the cylinder. One machine tool, John Wilkinson's boring machine, met that challenge by

Improvements in the lathe made it possible to proportion the number of threads on a screw to its diameter.

Lathes:
See also
Volume 1 page 12
Volume 4 pages 50-51

Entrepreneurs seized on the opportunity to sell such new devices as power saws, planers, and borers.

precisely manufacturing cylinders for Watt's engine (see Volume 2). It was one of many machine tools that opened up new manufacturing possibilities.

During the early years of the Industrial Revolution inventors took an ancient invention, the lathe, and added many improvements. The new design held the cutting tool in a fixed position by use of a slide rest, allowing more precise, complex,

A MATTER OF NUTS AND BOLTS

Henry Maudslay was born in Woolwich in 1771. His father worked at the Woolwich Arsenal. Maudslay's father apprenticed him to a lock manufacturer. Young Maudslay soon exhibited mechanical talent and rose to foreman. When his boss refused to increase his pay, Maudslay quit to start his own business.

His first independent job was to build machinery for a factory that produced pulleys for ships. Over the next 30 years Maudslay invented a number of machines that were essential to the Industrial Revolution. The most famous was a metal lathe that produced standardized nuts and bolts, something that had never been done before. Until Maudslay invented his lathe, every nut and bolt was a specialty product. A half-inch nut manufactured in one shop would not tightly fit a half-inch bolt manufactured somewhere else. Even nuts and bolts manufactured in the same shop might not fit. If the specific nut that had been made to fit a specific bolt was misplaced, endless confusion ensued. Maudslay's invention ended this confusion and inefficiency. His contributions to the machine tool industry were critical to the progress of the Industrial Revolution.

Maudslay was the first British engineer to appreciate how a machine shop needed absolutely precise tools in order to manufacture precise parts. Toward that end he developed precise machine **jigs** that had surfaces so perfectly smooth that when one surface was placed atop another, the two surfaces could only be separated by sliding them apart. In other words, there was no gap between the surfaces to let in a knife or chisel. Such precision had never before been achieved. Maudslay also perfected a measuring machine that was accurate to within 0.0001 inch. This was a stupendous achievement for his time. His other inventions included methods for printing calico cloth and desalting seawater from ship's boilers, and a number of stationary and marine engines.

Skilled machinists had once relied on hand tools to do their precision work (opposite). Even large nuts and bolts were made on machine jigs to ensure a consistent fit.

JIG: a pattern piece, usually of metal, used as a guide for shaping and duplicating an object with a power tool

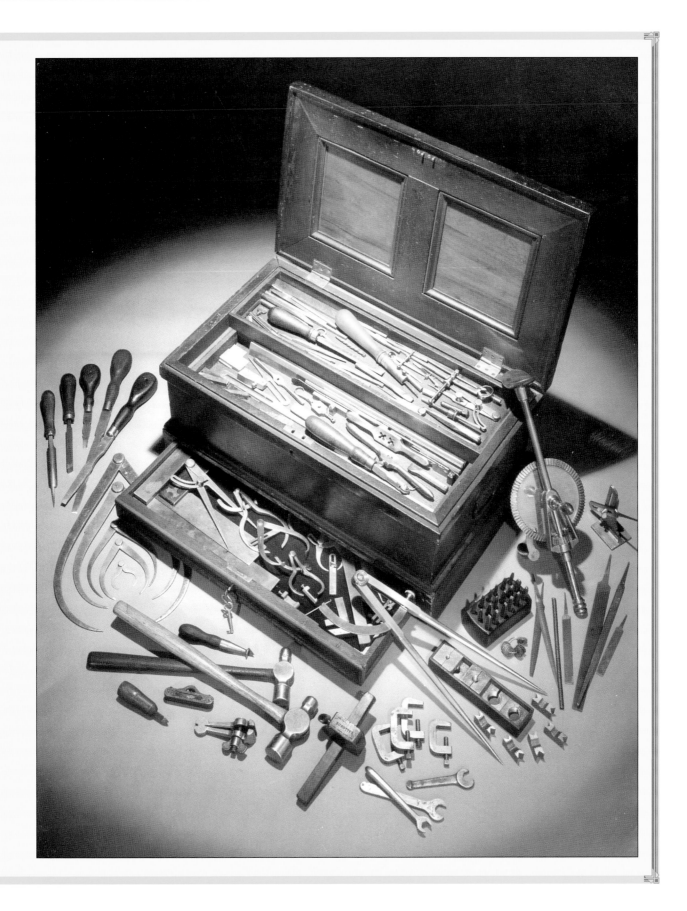

and reproducible work. This last feature was important because it meant that parts could be manufactured to a uniform standard. Similar advances were made with drill presses, shapers, grinders, and planers. The size of some machine tools also grew beyond simple hand tools to utilize water and steam power.

Because iron manufacture was becoming more efficient, the cost of iron declined. Inventors began to use iron to replace wood in everything from simple household utensils to complex, moving industrial machine parts. That trend, in turn, required better machine tools to do the necessary cutting, shaping, drilling, and planing. Craftsmen developed tools to do to metal what in the past had only been done to wood. The resultant developments throughout the machine tool industry both allowed the manufacture of some of the key inventions of the Industrial Revolution and accelerated the pace of change. For example, Wilkinson's boring machine was essential to build Watt's steam engine, which, in turn, produced a new source of power, which led to an increase in the number of machine tools required to manufacture engines and related parts. The machine tool industry was another example of how advances worked in mutually supporting ways where one sector stimulated another sector to change and grow, creating new opportunities everywhere.

The old world in which slow and gradual change from the tried and true ruled, the world where intelligent guesses and the rule-of-thumb held sway, gave way to innovation based on machine tool precision.

More sophisticated and accurate machine tools enabled engineers to make machinery to drive the rapid expansion of industry. This great steam engine powered a rolling mill for the manufacture of steel.

MACHINE TOOLS FOR MASS PRODUCTION

Between 1793 and 1815 Great Britain fought a series of wars against France. The sailing ships of the Royal Navy were Great Britain's most important military resource. Naturally, the British Admiralty was interested in using some manufacturing innovations to build warships.

Seamen manipulated sails through a complex rigging system that utilized blocks and tackle. In 1808 an inventor, Marc I. Brunel, patented a block-making machine. The "father of the English machine tool industry," Henry Maudslay, constructed the machine. The Admiralty set up a factory to use Brunel's device. It consisted of 45 machines of 22 different types capable of producing 100,000 wooden blocks a year. While in the past specialist craftsmen used hand tools to make blocks, unskilled workers could use Brunel's machine and do more than ten times as much work. The Admiralty's block-making factory was the first large-scale facility to use machine tools for mass production.

The Royal Navy was critical to Great Britain's defense. The navy's ships depended on efficient use of wind energy and the ability to quickly raise and lower sails. A British factory used machines built by Henry Maudslay to shape blocks for block and tackle on Royal Navy ships.

LIGHT AND POWER

Above: Imitators copied and sold Argand's oil lamp design, with its hollow wick and glass chimney, before he could profit from it.

COAL GAS: gas produced by burning coal, used as a fuel for lighting

Right: As early as 1792, William Murdock had devised a system to light his home with coal gas.

LIGHTING THE WORLD

Throughout most of the 1700s the candles and lamps people used for interior lighting needed frequent attention while providing a weak light with much smoke. In 1784 a Swiss inventor, François Ami Argand, introduced his new oil-burning lamp. It had three innovations: a hollow wick that supplied enriched air to allow the flame to burn hotter (thus reducing smoke) and brighter; a glass cylinder that worked like a chimney to give steady brightness; and a device that raised and lowered the wick and thus controlled brightness. The Argand burner dramatically increased interior lighting and proved to be an essential household item during most of the next century. On a larger scale it was used in lighthouses along the sea coast.

The next innovation involved gas lighting. A French inventor, Philippe Lebon, introduced wood gas lighting in 1801. The first public exhibition took place at a Parisian hotel where one of Lebon's lamps illuminated and warmed an interior room while another lit the outdoor garden. In turn an English inventor, William Murdock (who worked for the Boulton and Watt plant—see Volume 2), learned of Lebon's work and began to investigate all aspects of gas lighting.

Murdock made important advances, most notably the substitution of **coal gas** for wood gas. He devised a system in which the coal gas flowed into an outlet pipe and then through a network of piping to the site to be illuminated. One night in 1802 he lighted the entire Boulton and Watt factory. That meant the workers could operate machines during the hours of

Boulton and Watt factory:
See also
Volume 2 page 31

Murdock's system for producing the coal gas to light the Boulton and Watt factory: The coal was heated in the large metal chamber until it decomposed and produced gas, which then rose into the smaller vertical pipe and flowed through additional pipes to lamps throughout the factory building. Interior lighting allowed a factory to run 24 hours a day.

darkness and led to night shifts for factories where machinery ran continuously.

Gas lighting spread quickly. In 1806 Murdock illuminated a textile factory. The next year a commercial company introduced street lighting by gas. By 1820 entire city streets were lit by gas, as were factories, theaters, and even some private homes.

Murdock's accomplishment demonstrated the basis for an amazing future: a central source provided the gas that flowed

Gaslights light up a mail coach in a London street in 1827.

through pipes to the place where consumers burned it to light their buildings. This was a supply "network" that served as a model for later systems, including water, sewage, electric power, and the telephone.

BRINGING LIGHT UNDERGROUND

The Society for Preventing Accidents in Coal Mines enlisted the great English chemist Sir Humphry Davy to investigate the conditions leading to mine explosions. Davy replied, "If you

Sir Humphry Davy discovered that underground coal mine explosions were caused by accumulations of volatile **methane** gas being ignited by the heat of miners' lamps.

METHANE: an odorless, easy to ignite gas that occurs naturally in coal mines and oil wells

13

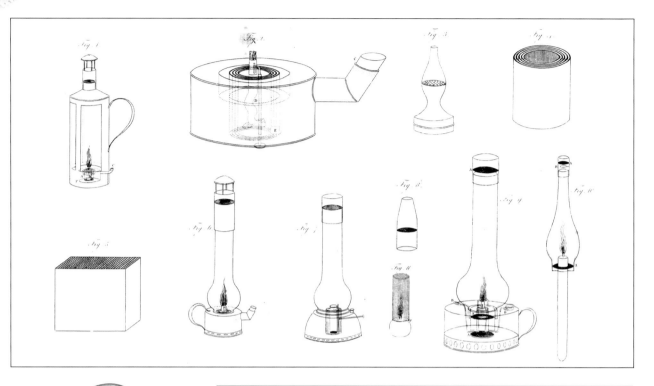

Above: Davy needed only three months to design several versions of a safety lamp that burned with less heat and so would not ignite methane gas.

Left: An example of the style of Davy lamp that was still used in coal mines until the 1950s.

think my visiting the mines can be of any use, I will cheerfully do so." In 1816 Davy produced a lamp that improved safety, although mining remained an exceedingly dangerous occupation.

THE ROTARY ENGINE

Until 1781 all engines were reciprocating pumping machines. Back in 1777 the ironmaster John Wilkinson (see Volume 2) had asked Watt to develop an engine that could drive the huge hammers used in an iron forge. Watt experimented with different designs and concluded that it was necessary to invent some method to convert the back-and-forth action of the steam piston into rotary (or turning) motion. Watt designed a crankshaft to accomplish this conversion. However, he was so occupied with setting up his steam engines that he failed to register a patent. An employee stole his idea and patented it. When Watt returned to the challenge of converting back-and-forth action into rotary motion, he did not fight the crankshaft patent. Instead, Watt designed something better—a system of rotating wheels.

Watt held a patent on his low-pressure steam engine until 1800. Up until that year he successfully blocked rival designs. The design that best competed with Watt's engine was a high-pressure engine. High-pressure engines worked on the difference between elevated, or high pressure, in a cylinder and a vacuum. Once Watt's patent ran out, inventors could work to bring high-pressure engines to the market.

The first to do so successfully was Richard Trevithick. Trevithick built a working high-pressure steam engine in 1802. It turned out that there were market niches for both low- and high-pressure steam engines. Watt's low-pressure engines were commonly used in manufacturing. High-pressure engines were commonly used in mining and transportation. Trevithick labored hard to adapt his high-pressure engine to the requirements of an exciting new mode of transportation, the railroad.

Above: James Watt dominated steam engine production from about 1769 until 1800. During that period nearly 500 Watt steam engines were built. Most of those Watt engines powered water pumps.

Trevithick built a full-size working model of his railroad and his "Catch-Me-Who-Can" steam engine, which could travel at 12 miles per hour.

THE TRANSPORTATION REVOLUTION

Around the British Isles hundreds of small ships carried freight between ports. The areas around the major ports had decent roads. Farther inland the few roads that existed were in poor condition. Consequently, until the spread of railroads strings of packhorses or horse-drawn carts carried nearly all the inland trade.

Industrialization and the rapid growth of urban areas required supplies of heavy, bulky raw materials such as coal and iron. Transport costs influenced the market for those items. Close to a mine coal was cheap but quickly became expensive the farther away from the mine it was. Coal and many other products could not seek wider markets until the transportation system improved.

ROADS AND CANALS

When Imperial Rome abandoned Britain in the fourth century, it left behind a good road network. Centuries of neglect

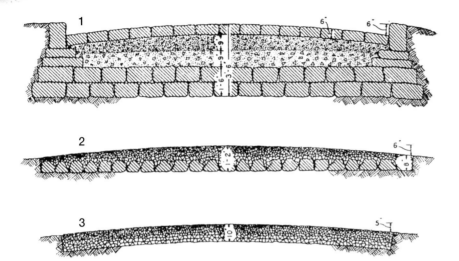

Cross section of an ancient Roman roadbed (1) compared to an 1820 English road of compacted gravel over large stones (2) and an 1816 English Macadam road made entirely of compacted gravel (3).

followed. As a result, when the Industrial Revolution began, few areas had decent roads. A politician who lived on the outskirts of London wrote, "The road is grown so infamously bad that we live here in the same solitude as we should do if cast on a rock in the middle of the ocean, and all the Londoners tell me that there is between them and us a great impassable gulf of mud." Along such roads columns made up of hundreds of draft animals—horses, donkeys, mules—hauled

Large stones were hauled from the quarry to the roadside, where laborers broke them up into smaller pieces.

wagons and carts or carried baskets strapped across their backs to move goods around the countryside. The going was slow—a loaded wagon did well if it covered 15 miles a day— and expensive, since the drivers and the animals required food and care.

To encourage road improvements, Parliament permitted the creation of local companies, or trusts. A group of merchants and landowners would apply to Parliament for permission to be responsible for building and repairing a road between two points. If Parliament approved, the trustees were allowed to place toll gates at each end of their road. The tolls were supposed to provide a profit for the investors and to cover the costs of maintaining the road.

The improved roads benefited merchants and landowners, but the requirement to pay tolls angered many others. A magazine described a typical protest: "...between ten and eleven at night a prodigious body of Somersetshire people came with drums beating and loud shouts, armed with cutting instruments fixed in long staves etc., and some disguised in women's apparel, and demolished the turnpike." It was the third time the turnpike had been attacked over a span of three days.

In spite of such opposition, the turnpike trusts continued to work to provide decent roads. By 1820 the trusts were operating about 21,000 miles of road. The carriage trade (horse-drawn vehicles, including carriages and coaches, the bus and taxi service of their time) responded by offering lighter, faster, and better sprung (to reduce bumping) coaches to convey travelers. Travel times were slashed. In 1780 a traveler required four to five days to go from London to Manchester, a distance of about 170 miles; by 1820 the journey required one and a half days. London to Edinburgh, Scotland (about 350 miles), had taken 10 days in summer and 12 in winter. In 1830 a carriage company advertised a travel time of 42 hours 33 minutes!

The eighteenth-century British economist Adam Smith wrote that "Good roads, by diminishing the expense of carriage, put the remote parts of the country more nearly upon a level with ...the town. They are upon that account the greatest of all improvements."

The improvements came about in part because the trusts frequently hired engineering specialists to design the roads and supervise construction. The celebrated John McAdam (for whom the tarry road surface "macadam" is named) was one such specialist. McAdam emphasized the need for a firm

ALL ROADS LEAD TO LONDON

London was the political capital, the center from which overseas enterprise was financed, and the center to which new wealth from foreign trade flowed. Quite simply, London dominated Great Britain's economic life.

During the 1700s London contained about 10 percent of the nation's population. Just feeding London was a great task. The surrounding area had to provide London with food. Each morning the roads leading to London filled with horse-drawn carts carrying food and other goods to the capital.

London itself was an important center for manufacturing, including food processing and the making of

furniture and clothing. London's population and industry, in turn, required all sorts of consumer goods and tools such as pots and pans, timber, and nails. London was also the hub for collecting and distributing a large amount of the nation's inland trade.

Almost all inland trade routes led to London. Moreover, London was the center for foreign trade, with most imports and exports moving through the port of London.

The Thames River provided London's link with oceangoing trade.

road base and insisted on meticulous construction techniques. His reward came in 1815 when the government appointed him surveyor-general for all British roads.

In addition to making travel much easier, the new roads provided economic benefits by opening up new markets and linking producers and consumers more efficiently. But it was still much easier to move heavy goods by water than by land. Wealthy landowners and businessmen earned much of their money by exploiting the mineral deposits, particularly coal, that lay beneath their land. To make a really good profit, they had to find ways to transport heavy loads easily and cheaply. That search led to the construction of a canal system and a period of speculation called "canal mania."

Canals:
See also
Volume 5 pages 13-15, 18

CANALS

As was the case with turnpikes, canal construction was done by local initiative responding to local conditions. In 1759 the Duke of Bridgewater hired the engineering genius James Brindley to build a canal to transport coal from his pits at Worsley to the market at Manchester. Bridgewater's 10-mile-long canal cost the huge sum of 350,000 pounds (about $600,000). Yet it quickly proved a great economic success, reducing the cost of coal in Manchester by half and earning a

Below: England's first canal opened in 1757 and was used for transporting coal. A single horse, which could haul only two tons in a wagon, could tow a canal barge with a 50-ton load.

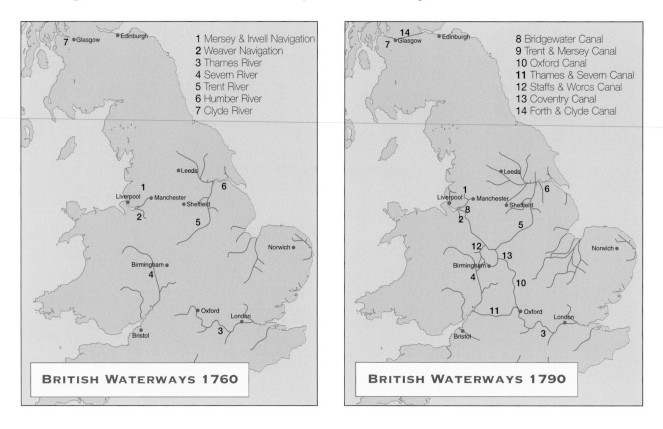

1 Mersey & Irwell Navigation
2 Weaver Navigation
3 Thames River
4 Severn River
5 Trent River
6 Humber River
7 Clyde River

8 Bridgewater Canal
9 Trent & Mersey Canal
10 Oxford Canal
11 Thames & Severn Canal
12 Staffs & Worcs Canal
13 Coventry Canal
14 Forth & Clyde Canal

BRITISH WATERWAYS 1760

BRITISH WATERWAYS 1790

tremendous profit for the duke. An observer reported, "This mine had lain dormant in the bowels of the earth from time immemorial...on account of the price of land carriage which was so excessive that [the coal] could not be sold at a reasonable cost."

In 1763 Bridgewater had the canal extended to link England's rapidly expanding textile manufacturing region with the port of Liverpool. Bridgewater's success stimulated a nationwide surge of canal construction that led to many benefits. New

Below: Until the perfection of steam engines human or animal teams provided the power to haul barges along the canals. Some canals handsomely rewarded investors. For example, the Trent and Mersey canal yielded a profit of 75 percent. Others worked out less well and earned investors nothing.

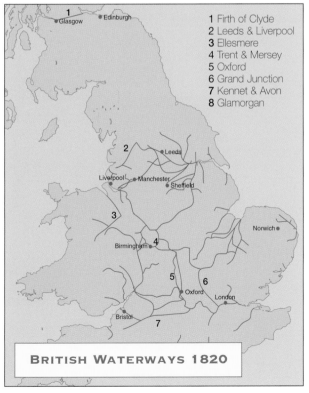

1 Firth of Clyde
2 Leeds & Liverpool
3 Ellesmere
4 Trent & Mersey
5 Oxford
6 Grand Junction
7 Kennet & Avon
8 Glamorgan

BRITISH WATERWAYS 1820

canals connected the industrial Midlands (central England) with London and with coastal ports. Canals also opened up trade with places that were often isolated when bad weather made the roads impassable. Old towns were revitalized and new ones established. The prices of numerous goods declined since canal transport was one-quarter to one-half as expensive as road transport.

Few investors were as wealthy as Bridgewater, who had financed the canal out of his own pocket. Consequently, investors cooperated with other partners to undertake new projects. At that time what was called a joint stock company (a

corporation formed with capital from multiple investors who jointly own the company's stock) was technically illegal. However, investors often found clever lawyers or obliging politicians to help them evade the law. As a result, many canal companies were joint stock companies and were even able to advertise openly for investors. By 1792 canal mania had reached such a fevered pitch in the port of Bristol that the proposed canal "was enthusiastically supported by influential persons, and a very large sum was subscribed [pledged] by those present, who struggled violently with each other in their rush to the subscription book."

Canal locks served to raise or lower water levels so canal barges could ascend or descend a waterway.

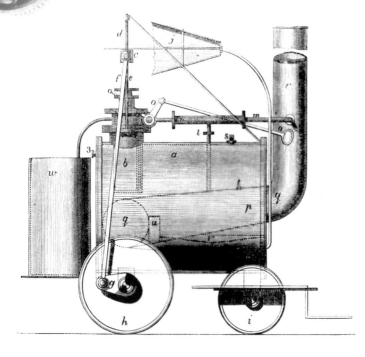

Above: Side view of Richard Trevithick's locomotive, powered by a high-pressure steam engine.

Below: Horse-drawn mining wagons, whose railed tracks led directly to the first railroads.

Of course, such passion sometimes led to unwise investment, a behavior that would repeat itself when the railroad boom began. But the canal boom showed that investors were willing and able to secure large amounts of capital and invest it in long-term projects. This marriage of money and investors was vital in promoting large transportation and industrial projects.

In addition to providing economic benefits, the canal movement gave rise to a new breed of engineers called civil engineers. They, and the workers who developed their talents building the canals, would provide the required skill when a new, revolutionary mode of transportation swept the nation.

THE RAILROADS

The first railroads, using animal or human power, began operating in mines around the middle of the sixteenth century. By 1800

improvements in metallurgy allowed the construction of more railroads. Most continued to be used in and around mines, and used cast or wrought-iron rails. Horses hauled wheeled carts along the tracks, or a fixed steam engine pulled a cable that was attached to the cart. Since ironmakers could not yet produce rails strong enough to support the weight of a locomotive, most people regarded these early railroads as little more than a useful but nonessential addition to the existing road and canal network.

In 1803 the inventor of the high-pressure steam engine, Richard Trevithick, made a locomotive capable of pulling 25 tons at four miles an hour. (A loaded horse-drawn wagon could haul a fraction of that amount at about two miles an hour.) That was a very impressive technical achievement; but before steam locomotives entered widespread use, certain

Railroads:
See also
Volume 5 pages 28, 30-41

Left: In addition to his work on locomotives George Stephenson invented a safety lamp for coal mining.

Below: A commemorative jug depicting a steam locomotive pulling a train of freight wagons.

PAST

FIRST LOCOMOTIVE   THE ROCKET

Rd. 72397.   WOVEN IN PURE SILK BY T. STEVENS, COVENTRY.   Rd. 72397.

PRESENT

George Stephenson,

THE PIONEER OF RAILWAYS.

problems had to be solved. The flimsy track caused frequent derailments. Indeed, derailments were so common that after Trevithick demonstrated his third locomotive, "Catch-Me-Who-Can," in 1808 and it eventually derailed, he abandoned the field. Some people asserted that horses could move carts along the rails more efficiently than steam engines. Because mobile steam engines were just being developed, this claim had some merit.

The Stockton and Darlington Railway began operation in 1825 and was the first to carry passengers along with freight. Its first locomotive was the "Locomotion," designed by the great pioneer railroad and locomotive builder George Stephenson. However, tracks were still too weak, and locomotives were unreliable and expensive to operate. The Stockton and Darlington remained best suited for hauling coal and other minerals at low speeds. At times it even reverted to horse-drawn rail cars.

The debate about horse power or steam power continued until 1829, when a public contest among competing locomotives took place on a section of track called the "Rainhill level." Stephenson's "Rocket," with its more efficient boiler design, proved superior. Thereafter steam engines improved so rapidly that within 10 years it was clear to everyone that steam locomotives were the path to the future.

Around the time the "Rocket" won the Rainhill competition, another key breakthrough occurred; the manufacture of the first so-called "fish belly," rolled iron edge rail. The rail bellied

A jigsaw puzzle displaying a picture of the Liverpool and Manchester Railway, which opened in 1830.

out on the underside to provide even resistance all along its length to a wheel riding along its surface and was much stronger than cast-iron rails. The fish-belly rails were strong enough to support the weight of heavier, more powerful locomotives.

In 1830 the Liverpool and Manchester Railway began operation with the "Rocket" working as the locomotive. This line's success marked the beginning of the railroad era and triggered a frenzy of railway construction throughout England. Each subsequent year brought something new: 1836, the first public passenger service to London; 1838, the London-to-Birmingham line fully open; 1840, London to Southampton; 1841, the Great Western from London to Bristol. Between

Railroad engineers cared about form as well as function. An elegant Moorish arch graced the route of the Liverpool and Manchester Railway.

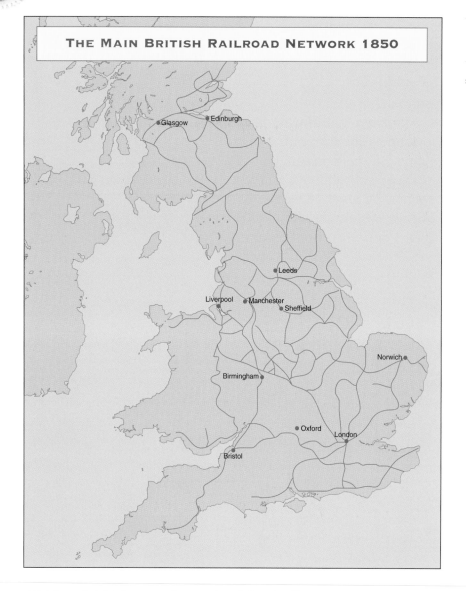

THE MAIN BRITISH RAILROAD NETWORK 1850

By 1855 Great Britain had some 8,000 miles of railroad track.

1844 and 1846 came the peak of the "railway mania" in Great Britain, with Parliament authorizing the construction of over 400 new lines.

The railroads had enormous economic and social consequences. For the first time in history there was a means of overland transportation that was hardly affected by weather conditions, relatively inexpensive, and capable of rapidly carrying large volumes of freight and passengers.

STEAM POWER TAKES TO THE WATER

After James Watt built the improved steam engine, various inventors took up the challenge of building steamboats. Among them was the American John Fitch, who built several demonstration steamboats between 1787 and 1790. The first

The American inventor Robert Fulton worked in France and England before returning to America to build the *Clermont* in 1807.

Steamboats:
See also
Volume 5 pages 19-26

steamboats employed crude methods to convert the piston rod's reciprocating motion (moving alternately back and forth) to the rotary motion needed to turn a paddle wheel. The required technical breakthrough came in Scotland, when William Symington introduced a crank to convert linear to rotary motion. Symington employed his crank on the first commercially successful steam-powered boat in 1801, which was used as a canal tugboat.

Two years later another American, Robert Fulton, demonstrated a steamboat in France but failed to attract investors. Fulton's next effort came on the Hudson River in 1807 when his steamboat the *Clermont* demonstrated an average speed of five miles per hour. After a few improvements Fulton's vessel entered regular service between Albany and New York City. Steamboats proved enormously useful on the major American waterways and helped bring prosperity to its western frontier.

Meanwhile, other inventors made enduring contributions to

steam engineering, but the public remained suspicious. Boiler explosions and assorted collisions and wrecks did not help. In 1819 a sea captain and engineer named Moses Rogers built the steam powered *Savannah* for travel across the Atlantic. The *Savannah* had many innovative features: coal-fired instead of wood-fired boiler; seawater for boiler feed; collapsible paddle wheels in the event of dangerous storms. But people were afraid to cross the ocean on this new type of vessel, so the *Savannah* completed its first trans-Atlantic crossing, from the United States to Great Britain, without

passengers and without freight. Although the *Savannah* proved a financial failure, it showed the way to the future. Twenty years later some 776 steam-powered ships were registered in the British Isles alone.

Additional technical improvements were needed before steam-powered ocean travel boomed. They would come in the late 1830s. Meanwhile, steam-powered vessels demonstrated their value on canals and rivers worldwide. They provided one more link in an expanding transportation network that was moving people and freight faster and cheaper than ever before.

Steam-powered vessels on the Clyde River, which runs through the industrial city of Glasgow, Scotland.

THE REST OF EUROPE

Continental Europe watched Great Britain's Industrial Revolution with amazement, jealousy, and in some cases fear as well as hope. The astonishing occurrence of a number of inventions in a short period of time amazed European observers. The way they transformed Great Britain's economic position in relation to Europe was a source of envy. The revolution inspired a fear within the aristocracy and upper classes that Continental Europe might experience dramatic social change that would threaten their authority. Simultaneously, many in the middle and lower classes welcomed the chance to increase income and improve their lives. Last, the possibility of social revolution gave wonderful hope to those who wanted to overturn a society that they detested for its inequality.

Europe also faced some vexing natural obstacles that stood in the way of industrialization. Its countries were larger, and

The French built their canal system in an effort to solve the nation's poor and costly internal transport system.

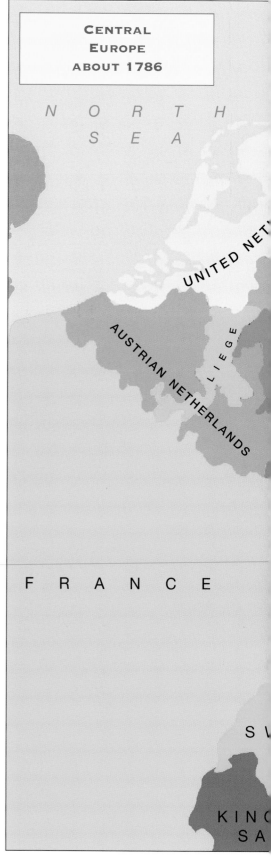

CENTRAL EUROPE ABOUT 1786

NORTH SEA

UNITED NET

AUSTRIAN NETHERLANDS

LIEGE

FRANCE

S

KIN
SA

BALTIC SEA

HOLSTEIN

RÜGEN

Hither Pomerania

PRUSSIA

MECKLENBURG

BREMEN

HANOVER

BRANDENBURG

POLAND

MÜNSTER

SILESIA

HESSE-CASSEL

OGNE

SAXONY

ÈVES

NASSAU

DARMSTADT

BOHEMIA

PALATINATE

WURTEMBURG

BAVARIA

AUSTRIA

HUNGARY

TYROL

SALZBURG

TZERLAND

The territory of the
modern nation of
Germany once consisted
of some 17 independent
states.

OM OF
INIA

VENETIAN
REPUBLIC

35

size, combined with difficult terrain, separated markets from one another and caused high transportation costs. Although Great Britain relied heavily on sea transport, on the continent only the Netherlands could do the same. Repeated wars had destroyed the shipping capacity of the other European nations. The others tried to use inland waterways as much as possible, but summer drought and winter flood made river transport less reliable.

Man-made obstacles also impeded industrial growth. Where there were roads, there were numerous toll stations. The tolls were often so high that shippers went to remarkable lengths to avoid paying. Political boundaries likewise imposed costs as each duchy, archduchy, bishopric, principality, and free city collected taxes and set its own rules on trade. Nations like Germany, Belgium, and Italy were a patchwork of such small political units. Even within a unified nation adherence to traditional business habits and resistance to change discouraged modernization.

Moreover, compared to Great Britain, Europe's poor were significantly worse off. A British traveler, Arthur Young, described rural France in the 1790s. In addition to meeting many beggars, he saw that "country girls and women are

A British cartoon in 1792 contrasted the poverty of France with the wealth of England. It shows a poor but happy Frenchman and an overfed, complaining Englishman.

FRENCH LIBERTY.

BRITISH SLAVERY.

without shoes or stockings; and the ploughmen at their work have neither sabots [wooden shoes] nor feet to their stockings." Young concluded: "This is poverty, that strikes at the root of national prosperity."

Another significant difference between Great Britain and the rest of Europe was the nature of the business firm. In Great Britain an industrial venture was a means to make money. New machines and methods were to be used intelligently to increase profits. In contrast, business firms on the continent were often family activities, closely managed and controlled by family members with power passed on from one generation to the next. The main goal of such family firms was to make possible a way of life by which the son could live as well as his father. Therefore, European family firms were often unwilling to take new risks connected with invention and innovation or to accept outside investment (since investors might interfere with family goals). Without outside investment they could not make the necessary capital expenditures to purchase the steam engines and power looms that powered the Industrial Revolution in England.

Also, nature and history had formed peoples outside of Great Britain who had different memories and different hopes. They had more recently known war in their backyards, remembered or still knew tyranny in their capitals. Such memories sometimes made people more conservative and less willing to take on the risks of invention and innovation.

Within Europe the Industrial Revolution spread first to Great Britain's closest neighbors. The early followers experienced some similarities in the way they industrialized; most notably the same industries (textiles, iron, coal mining) were modernized first. However, each nation in Europe followed its own path and pace toward industrialization. None precisely followed the unique path taken by the first pioneer, Great Britain.

BELGIUM

Great Britain unsuccessfully tried to maintain a monopoly over the inventions and innovations associated with the beginning of the Industrial Revolution. The British monopoly could not endure because Britons saw opportunity for profit in other countries, and foreigners sought to lure British industry to their own countries. The spread of the Industrial Revolution to western Europe began in Belgium. Belgium had long experience in the textile and metal trades. Consequently, as had occurred in Great Britain, the transformation of the Belgian economy centered on those industries.

REVOLUTION AND WAR

The French Revolution of 1789 was one of the most important events of modern history. Historians identify this revolution as the true starting point of the age of nationalism and European democracy. The French Revolution also triggered a series of wars that continued, with only a few breaks, until 1815. These wars had massive social and economic consequences.

After the French revolutionary government executed the French king, Louis XVI, military conflict began in 1792 when the French Republic declared war on Austria. The conflict eventually grew to include every European power. A major reason the struggle was so bitterly contested stemmed from the French challenge against the claim of dynastic power that allowed a royal family to control a country from one generation to the next. France wanted to replace dynastic power with a concept of national existence based on the rights of common people, and the French Republic was willing to use war to make this change. All European monarchs, even the uniquely constitutional British monarchy (see Volume 1), saw the French challenge as a mortal threat to aristocratic privilege.

From 1792 to 1800 France lurched from one military crisis to another as various groupings of hostile European powers attacked. A military genius, Napoleon Bonaparte, seized control of the French government in 1799, and in 1804 he named himself emperor. The period of conflict from 1792 to 1815 came to be known as the Napoleonic Wars.

Great Britain fought against France during most of the time from 1793 until the defeat and overthrow of Napoleon in 1815. Its major military weapon was the Royal Navy, which it used to blockade France and its allies while capturing their colonies around the world. The blockade was extremely effective in stopping French and French-allied overseas trade. It proved ruinous for those countries such as the Netherlands that depended on foreign trade. Napoleon tried to counter the British naval blockade with a policy called "the

Wars:
See also
Volume 6 pages 38-39

Continental System," an economic blockade that ended all commerce between Britain and the Continent. Napoleon hoped that the Continental System would harm Great Britain economically by cutting connections to European markets while benefiting French industry and agriculture by eliminating British competition. Napoleon's plan failed because Great Britain was able to find new markets and exploit gaps in the economic blockade.

The Industrial Revolution was well under way in Great Britain when the wars began, but it had only started to reach western Europe. Some technology transfer continued in spite of the wars, but by and large, the military struggles retarded European industrialization. By war's end in 1815 Great Britain enjoyed a dominant economic position in Europe.

Right: Napoleon Bonaparte seized control of the French government in 1799 by ordering his troops to occupy the chambers of the ruling council.

Opposite: France's King Louis XVI goes to the guillotine.

In 1795 the wars of the French Revolution raged, and France invaded and annexed the territory that is modern Belgium. This upset all tradition and brought a new, liberal political and social order that raised high expectations. In addition, the French Republic (and later the empire under the control of Napoleon Bonaparte) provided an emerging large market for Belgian goods while offering protection against English competition. These facts provided incentives for Belgian capitalists to innovate, take risks, and invest in mechanization.

In 1798 a British emigrant technician, William Cockerill, contracted with a Belgian entrepreneur to build five mechanized wool-spinning mills in the city of Verviers. The economic advantages were easily apparent. Within 12 years only six out of a total of 144 firms had completely mechanized wool spinning, yet those six accounted for more than half of total output.

Unaffected by Napoleon's enmity, the British cotton industry continued to flourish. English factory workers operate machinery for drawing cotton fibers.

By the late 1700s industrialists in other nations imported English-made machinery for producing cotton. Whenever possible, European manufacturers tried to adopt British machines in order to compete with cheaper, machine-made British goods.

Also like Great Britain, Belgium possessed coal and iron resources. No area in Europe so quickly adopted steam as the Belgian coal region. Up to the year 1790, 39 steam engines had been installed to drain water from the mines. In 1807 the Cockerill family founded a factory for building machines at Liège that quickly expanded into a large industrial business involving coal mining, iron smelting, pig iron production, and metal processing and fabrication. The Cockerills brought to the continent Henry Cort's puddling method (see Volume 2) and later introduced the first modern blast furnace. Later still their factories at Liège manufactured the continent's first locomotive and first iron ships.

Naturally other capitalists sought to emulate the Cockerills's success. Between 1832 and 1835 new blast furnaces began operation around Liège. In turn that led to the development of new coal mines and the founding of numerous factories for pig iron processing and related metallurgical manufacturing.

Other iron ore and coal-rich regions in Belgium underwent similar development. With the help of English engineers the decade of the 1820s witnessed a tremendous expansion of heavy industry based on the newest English techniques.

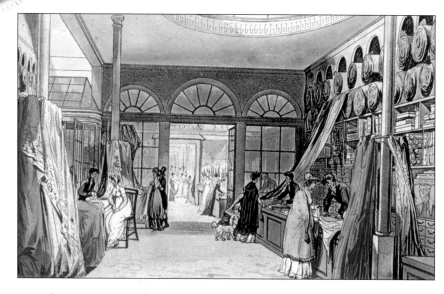

Left: An English fabric shop in the 1800s. People bought English textiles for their consistent quality.

Belgium in general, and the Flanders region in particular, had a long tradition of textile manufacture. In 1801, during an interval of peace between France and England, the son of a Ghent tanner, Liévin Bauwens, traveled to England to study English tanning methods. Instead, he learned more about the mechanization of the cotton industry. He returned to Ghent to establish a cotton-spinning factory using a device based on Crompton's mule (see Volume 2). Bauwens introduced additional English innovations and created a cotton-spinning family empire.

Other investors sought to duplicate Bauwens's success, most notably in the traditional calico-printing industry. The result was a large overinvestment that led to economic disaster when the Napoleonic Wars came to an end in 1815. After that year Belgian textiles faced direct competition from English textiles, and they could not meet the challenge. Consequently, textile growth was limited until the 1850s, when mechanization firmly took hold.

Overall, the combination of the wars of the French Revolution, the subsequent Napoleonic Wars, and political union with the Netherlands followed by separation slowed industrialization in Belgium. Eventually, the Belgian government took the initiative of building an "Iron Rhine" (named after the Rhine River, which was the economic spine of central Europe). The "Iron Rhine" was intended as a rail system to link Belgium's industries, its port at Antwerp, and Germany. Belgian banks made the long-term investment necessary to build the system, which provided the economic stimulus to continue Belgium's advance on the path of industrialization.

Historians consider Belgium to be the first follower of the British example of industrialization. More closely than any other nation, it installed copies of British inventions and innovations. That, combined with its iron and coal resources, allowed it to develop earlier and faster than other follower countries.

Ghent, Belgium, grew into a thriving commercial center. An early feat of industrial espionage was pulled off by Liévin Bauwens, who smuggled spinning and weaving machines and steam engines from England to his native city. Ghent was called "the Manchester of the continent." It was only natural therefore that the city desired to finally have a canal that would connect its port directly with the North Sea. A canal was dug from Ghent to Terneuzen. After its opening in 1827 sea-going vessels sailed into the city for the first time in its history.

THE INDUSTRIAL REVOLUTION COMES TO FRANCE

In 1780 France was a large, relatively wealthy country that had a work force skilled in traditional craftsmanship and a scientific community second to none. An outside observer might have predicted that France would rapidly embrace the Industrial Revolution and propel itself into a dominant economic position. Instead, political and military events controlled French affairs from the time of the French Revolution (1789) until the end of the Napoleonic Empire at the Battle of Waterloo in 1815. Those events prevented France from sharing fully the British inventions and innovations that drove the Industrial Revolution.

To preserve its economic advantages, Britain passed laws that banned the emigration of skilled craftsmen (to prevent them from teaching foreigners new industrial practices) and forbade the export of most types of machinery. Still, technology

Below left: James Hargreaves, the inventor of the spinning jenny, did not patent it. As a result, it was widely copied on both sides of the Atlantic Ocean, and Hargreaves failed to prosper from his brilliant invention.

transfers from Britain to France did take place before and during the Revolutionary and Napoleonic Wars (1792-1815). For example, in 1771 the son of a mastermind of French industrial espionage brought back from England drawings of the newly invented spinning jenny (see Volume 2). French manufacturers quickly built copies. British technical experts— skilled mechanics, foremen, engineers, entrepreneurs—came to France before the wars to sell their knowledge and played key roles in modernizing French industry.

In the 1780s the French government invited the British ironmaster John Wilkinson (see Volume 2) to serve as a technical adviser. Among various contributions Wilkinson recommended Le Creusot as a promising site to develop a modern ironworks. Likewise, during a peaceful interlude in

Industrial espionage:
See also
Volume 4 pages 23, 26, 29, 32

Below: In 1784 Le Creusot became the first place in France to use the rotary steam engine. It powered the hammers of the forge. The Creusot artillery workshop.

Inset: A Creusot cannon made around 1874.

1814 a Birmingham steel technician brought to France the crucible process for steel manufacture (see Volume 2).

THE SLOW SPREAD OF MODERN METHODS

While the war period slowed technology transfer, unique French characteristics also played their part in delaying modern industrialization. French population growth during the 1800s was considerably slower than in other European countries. The population rose 31 percent from 1800 to 1850, compared with a 46 percent rise in Germany and a 95 percent rise in Great Britain. Consequently, consumer demand within the home market was relatively smaller and provided less of a stimulus for mechanization.

Consider that in the 1780s France produced more iron than Great Britain. Thereafter France fell ever more behind. In part that was because France still had large forests to provide wood for **charcoal**. Many French ironmasters were first and foremost large landowners whose land included forests and who merely made iron as a side occupation. So French ironmasters had less incentive to adopt new methods based on **coke**.

In 1785 a blast furnace built to Wilkinson's specifications at Le Creusot became the first on the continent to operate using

CHARCOAL: a fuel made by charring wood in a buried fire so that very little air enters the fire

COKE: a form of coal that has been heated to remove gases so that it burns with great heat and little smoke

Charcoal:
See also
Volume 4 pages 62-63
Coke:
See also
Volume 2 page 35

Charcoal mounds in France. Charcoal producers piled dirt on large stacks of wood so that little air could get to the wood as it smoldered. The fire could not totally consume the wood, and what remained was charcoal.

coke. Le Creusot eventually grew into a great industrial combine, Schneider-Creusot. But by 1815 only one other facility had joined Le Creusot in producing coke-blast iron (iron produced in a blast furnace fueled by coke). Until 1856 charcoal furnaces produced more than half of all French iron. Instead of embracing the opportunity to adopt new techniques, French ironmasters preferred things the way they were. Indeed, French manufacturers of all types proved to be much more conservative and resistant to change than their English counterparts while emphasizing quality over quantity.

WATER POWER

Unlike Great Britain, France did not have rich coal resources and so had to import significant amounts of coal. Compared to Great Britain, it also had a much larger geographic area, which increased transport costs. Consequently, the coal-fueled steam engine did not offer French manufacturers the same advantages it provided their English counterparts. Instead, French industry relied heavily on water power.

French scientists had gathered a large body of theoretical knowledge about water power in the 1700s. During the 1800s they built on that knowledge and led the way in water-power improvements. Jean-Victor Poncelet invented an undershot waterwheel using curved vanes that provided a major technical

A French iron forge with a charcoal-fueled furnace. A French ironmaster traveled to England and observed modern puddling and rolling mills. What he saw amazed him: "Internal consumption is said to be 110,000 tons; a frightening quantity, but when one has gone through England it does not seem incredible."

WATER POWER

Since ancient times water power moved wheels in one of two ways. Either they were the more economical undershot mills, which simply immersed the bottom of the waterwheel in a stream, or the more powerful overshot mills, in which water was diverted from a stream to spill over the top of the waterwheel. In the 1750s the English engineer John Smeaton began an analysis of waterwheel performance that led to a revolutionary design that took water in the middle. He called it a breast wheel because he invented a casing, called the "breast," that prevented spillage. The breast thus allowed water to be taken in the middle of the wheel, combining the best features of the undershot and overshot mills.

Small improvements followed. Waterwheels and the machinery connected to them had always been mostly made from wood. Smeaton took the lead in adding metal parts that improved their strength. In 1776 Smeaton introduced the first cast-iron wheel and two years later cast-iron gearing. Several inventors came up with curved blades for the waterwheel that increased the efficiency of undershot wheels by 65 percent. Because of such technical improvements water power remained in use for decades after the introduction of steam power.

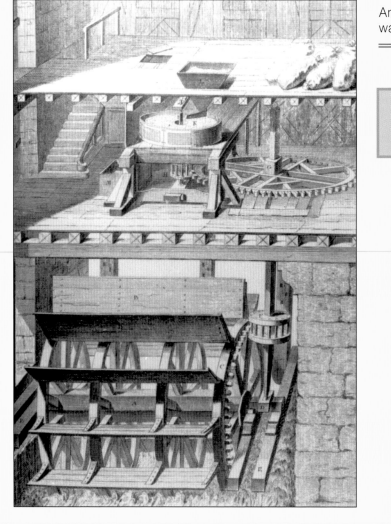

An undershot waterwheel, with water flowing under the wheel.

John Smeaton:
See also
Volume 2 page 35

breakthrough in 1823-1835. Curved vanes extracted more energy from the water's motion by keeping the water in contact with the wheel for a longer time. Another inventor, Benoit Fourneyron, patented the prototype of modern turbines in 1832. Turbines were lighter and smaller than waterwheels, but their curved blades were designed to extract much greater energy from water. Later versions used steam as their power source. Water power was so widespread that until the middle of the nineteenth century the cotton industry made only marginal use of steam power. As late as 1865, 60 percent of all industrial establishments outside of Paris and Lyons used water power, while only 31 percent relied on steam.

Another consequence of the lack of coal resources

Above and left: French artisans were known for their ornamental ribbons and braid.

was the French emphasis on fuel efficiency. In 1815 (after the wars) a British technician delivered a **compound engine** that achieved a 50 percent fuel savings compared to Watt's engine. Although the new type of engine was not popular in England, it spread rapidly in France. French technologists themselves devised many fuel-saving innovations, such as the recovery of hot gases from blast furnaces and the manufacture of high-pressure steam engines that were superior to British models.

FRENCH TEXTILES

Just as in metallurgy, French textiles failed to challenge English supremacy in mass production. Cotton mills were slow to

Water power:
See also
Volume 1 page 9
Volume 4 page 28

COMPOUND ENGINE: a steam engine that gets more work out of the steam by compressing it and allowing it to expand multiple times adopt jennies and water frames until a treaty in 1786 opened the French market to British cottons. Thereafter the cotton industry had to modernize to survive. Still, it was the quality and flair of French fine work, including ribbons, braid, lace, and belts, that set it apart from that of other nations. French textiles competed effectively with British products only in the luxury markets, and those markets were small compared to the mass markets dominated by Great Britain.

SLOW AND STEADY PROGRESS

After 1815 the pace of French industrialization accelerated. The French government contributed by directly sponsoring

THE JACQUARD LOOM AND THE BIRTH OF THE COMPUTER

In 1790 Joseph-Marie Jacquard developed an idea for a new loom. The turmoil and war brought on by the French Revolution prevented him from perfecting his idea. Instead, the 38-year-old inventor joined the revolutionaries in the defense of his home city of Lyons. The year 1801 brought a peaceful interval, and Jacquard demonstrated an improved **drawloom** that allowed intricate patterns to be woven into cloth. It used coded punch cards similar to modern machine-readable computer cards. The coded punch cards controlled the pattern that was printed onto a fabric. Rods reached out to the cards. When a rod sensed a hole in the card, it brought down another rod that put in place the correct colored yarn.

In 1806, Jacquard's loom was declared public property, and Jacquard received a pension from the government and royalties on each machine sold. The new device upset the silk weavers of Lyons, who feared it would deprive them of their jobs. These French "Luddites" (see Volume 2 for the British Luddite movement) burned looms and attacked Jacquard himself. But the loom was so clearly superior that by 1812 there were about 11,000 in use in France. It eventually spread to England during the 1820s and then worldwide. Jacquard's invention is the basis of the modern automatic loom.

The inventor of the modern computer, Charles Babbage, adopted Jacquard's brilliant breakthrough use of machine-readable cards. To honor Jacquard's contribution, Babbage owned a large portrait of Jacquard made of woven silk!

Charles Babbage, the inventor of the modern computer, used the principle underlying Jacquard's loom for his own analytical machine.

DRAWLOOM: a loom for the weaving of patterned cloth

industrial experimentation to a much greater degree than the British government. Yet France still lagged behind, as shown by the fact that French industries often installed British machinery that was considered obsolete in England. Also, while France was at war, England had gobbled up overseas markets and made it impossible for France later to rely on foreign trade to propel major industrialization. In addition France had a larger supply of low-wage labor than Great Britain, and that reduced the incentive for mechanization.

Although it had to rely mostly on the home market, France still made industrial progress, with textiles leading the way. Mechanization in cotton mills led to larger factories and

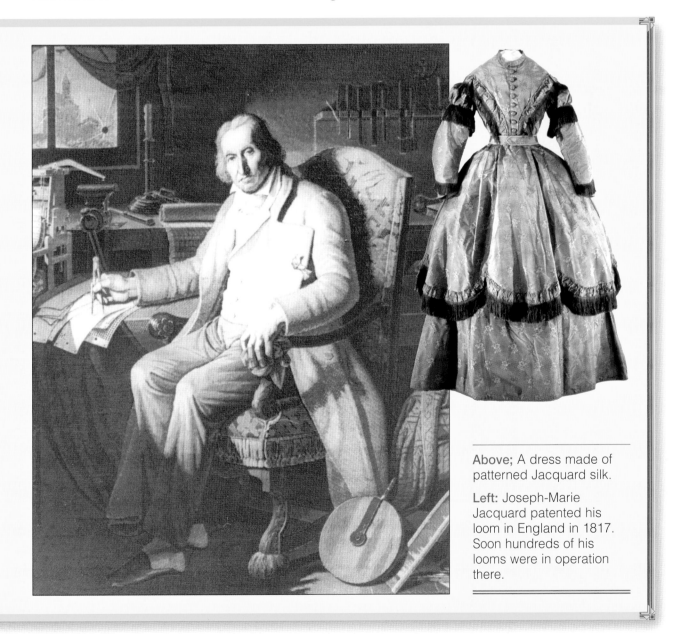

Above; A dress made of patterned Jacquard silk.

Left: Joseph-Marie Jacquard patented his loom in England in 1817. Soon hundreds of his looms were in operation there.

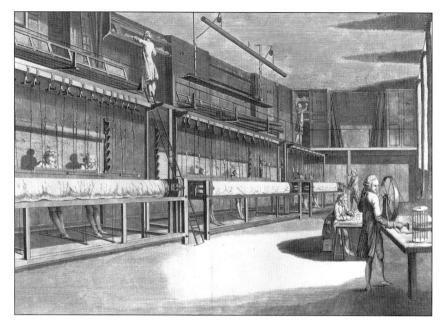

Top: An eighteenth-century Parisian textile workshop.

Above: A sample of French silk made during the eighteenth century.

greater production, with raw cotton consumption increasing fivefold from 1820 to 1860. By 1869 the French iron industry was the largest producer on the continent, although it was only one-quarter the size of the British iron industry.

As was the case everywhere, since the increased scale of industry required much higher capital investment, the number of producers declined. In 1815 France had some 1,000 small iron producers scattered around the country. After 1850 production was concentrated in 10 large firms that, combined, made more than half of French iron.

The story of French industrialization during the first half of the nineteenth century was one of slow, steady progress. Most exports were quality goods made with little mechanization in noncentralized cottage industries or by small workshop production. This narrow export market combined with limited coal resources and relatively slower population growth to limit industrial growth and incentive for modernization. Unlike England, France was also slow to urbanize, and the agricultural sector continued to contribute almost half of national income as late as midcentury.

By the end of the first period of the Industrial Revolution, around 1860, France was second only to Great Britain in industrial capacity. Yet compared to 1815, the gap had widened. Moreover, Germany was gaining fast in science, technology, and industrial might, and in 10 years would administer a terrible setback by badly defeating France in the Franco-Prussian War. France would emerge weak and shaken, and never again regain its top ranking among industrial powers.

THE INDUSTRIAL REVOLUTION IN GERMANY

As was the case in France, the Napoleonic Wars hit hard within the geographic area that became Germany. When peace came in 1815, there was no German nation in the modern sense but rather Prussia (roughly the area from the Polish border to a little west of Berlin) and a collection of smaller German states. That situation did not change until the Wars of German Unification in the 1860s, which climaxed with the Franco-Prussian War of 1870–1871.

The early industrial period in Germany, up to 1830, laid the groundwork for more rapid growth. Important institutional reforms occurred in agriculture, where the peasants became free, and the right to individual property in land and labor became established. In 1818 came the Prussian customs union that eliminated internal barriers to trade. No longer would a merchant have to pay tariffs when moving goods from city to city and through one of the many small German principalities that joined the union. This measure led first to a spate of road building and later to railroad construction. It also triggered banking reforms that addressed the problems of having numerous different currencies within the same trading zone.

As occurred worldwide, during the first phase of industrialization Germany "borrowed" industrial technology from abroad, particularly from Great Britain, and then German craftsmen set about making their own improvements. For example, a Scottish engineer who had learned about blast furnace operation while employed at the famous Carron Works in Scotland cooperated with two highly skilled German technicians to establish the first coke blast furnace in Germany in 1794–1796. But German

A German tannery of the 1800s.

A grape harvest in Germany.

industrialization moved at a slow pace until 1830, at which time it accelerated tremendously, driven, more so than elsewhere, by the expansion of railroads.

THE GERMAN RAILROAD BOOM

German railroad construction followed a series of growth cycles. To begin, railway construction required state approval in order to do such things as take land from private individuals for the tracks. In the late 1830s the Prussian government set procedures by which private companies could obtain the needed land. This removed a significant obstacle, and a building boom followed. The boom lasted until 1844, when the government established restrictive laws against speculative transactions in railroad securities (stocks, bonds, and the like). A commercial and financial crisis occurred in 1847-1848 followed by two years of political crisis caused by the revolution of 1848–1849.

Political stability returned after 1849, and the state allocated enormous sums for railroad construction. Simultaneously, the government retreated from close control of coal mining (which opened the way for entrepreneurial activity) and liberalized restrictions on the formation of joint stock industrial companies. A remarkable expansion of railroads followed and carried with it rapid growth in a range of heavy industries.

During the 1840s Prussian railroads expanded at a rate of 20 percent a year, while iron and coal increased at rates of 4 and 4.5 percent. Most iron rails were imported, and most domestic rails were made from imported pig iron. The profits for the Prussian factories that could meet some of the demand for iron were attractive enough to bring in large numbers of new investors. The resultant industrial development was so rapid that by the next decade Prussia was exporting rails while still expanding its domestic rail system at a rate of 10 percent per year. Furthermore, the demand for rail iron was so strong that it provided incentives to shift from the older charcoal technology to more efficient coke smelting and refining.

The railroad boom transformed Germany. Industrialists gained access to the nation's large coal and iron resources. The railroads stimulated vast

THE ZOLLVEREIN, OR GERMAN CUSTOMS UNION

When Prussia passed a law in 1818 to abolish internal customs dues, it also announced that it was ready for free trade with its neighbors. Governments relied on such customs dues to help cover their expenses, so they were reluctant to do without. Ten years passed before a neighboring state (Hesse-Darmstadt) decided to change its traditional habits and sign a free trade agreement with Prussia. Later in 1828 several south German states established a similiar customs union, and thereafter the practice spread.

In 1834 the Zollverein (a German word whose root refers to paying a toll) was established under Prussian leadership. Eighteen states joined the union to create a free trade area covering most of Germany. From an economic standpoint the Zollverein was a good thing because it eliminated barriers to trade and thus encouraged entrepreneurial activity, including investing in machinery and adopting innovation.

The customs union proved even more important from a political standpoint by uniting German-speaking peoples who lived in the many small German states and giving them a sense that they belonged to one nation. By 1867 all of Germany outside of Austria, except for the two city states of Hamburg and Bremen, belonged to the Zollverein. Historians came to realize that the creation of the German customs cnion had been an important step toward German unification.

investment in iron, steel, and coal mining, the movement of labor toward urban industry, and a significant increase in per capita (per person) productivity and income. Ahead, beginning in the late 1860s, lay an equally remarkable era of industrial growth when new technologies and organizational methods spread throughout the economy, and Germany passed France in industrial capacity and began to challenge Great Britain.

By the 1860s the largest, most modern German iron and steel factories served the needs of the railroads. A railroad bridge in Germany.

VON ROMBERG'S ENGINE

In 1788 a German aristocrat ordered a Newcomen engine (see Volume 2) for use in his mine in the Ruhr region. At that time the design of the Newcomen engine was 76 years old, but none had been installed in Germany. It took four years for all the engine's parts to arrive at the mine. By that time the mine owner decided he no longer wanted an engine. The parts lay in storage for eight years. Another German aristocrat, Frieherr von Romberg, bought the parts and had the engine installed at his own mine.

Meanwhile, a small number of Newcomen and Watt engines had been installed elsewhere in Germany. Typically the key components, such as the cylinders, were manufactured in England. Not until 1791 did German technicians manage to build an entire engine using German made parts.

Von Romberg's engine was an example of the slow pace of technology transfer in many areas of Europe and contrasts notably with the speed with which many entrepreneurs in Great Britain adopted new inventions and innovations.

Before the importation of steam engines German mines operated much as they always had. A sixteenth-century German mine relying on horses and carts.

GERMAN PEASANT LIFE DURING THE INDUSTRIAL REVOLUTION

As was the case throughout Europe, most rural German families depended on home manufacture to survive. A series of European wars took place through most of the early years of the Industrial Revolution. A nation's need for soldiers placed enormous stresses on the rural poor. In 1765 a German writer wrote, "In case of emergency [war], one man may be recruited out of two or three peasant families to protect the Fatherland without doing injury to agricultural production. This is hardly possible with families weaving woolen cloth. Their manufactures are like a machine consisting of many wheels which may not be touched."

Even during times of peace many rural families lived on the edge of poverty. A German writer described home manufacture in the preindustrial period:

"In bad times the longest working day does not suffice; the weavers who have between two and four dependent children fall heavily into debt and must regularly resort to poor relief. Only when two or three children sit at the loom can debts be repaid and savings made. If the brothers and sisters remain within the family and conduct an orderly economy, this offers a period when savings are possible. It is obvious how important it is to the parents to make their children work as early as possible, for they will not remain with them for long; the sons often marry at 22–23, the daughters at 18-19, both leave their parents and deliver them and their younger brothers and sisters into destitution. With the birth of children, the parents become poor; with their maturation, they become rich; and with the marriage, they fall back into misery."

Even the railroad boom did not greatly alter German peasant life. A writer described a peasant's home life in 1853: "If one enters the cottages of those rural dwellers, who do not hold large pieces of land and who have to gain their basic subsistence by spinning, one often finds the whole family sitting at the spinning wheel...grandmother, mother and grandchild are occupied with spinning, whereas the father and his grown-up son work in the field or do other jobs around the house, such as prepare the meals, clean turnips or peel potatoes, if and as long as they have any. In the weavers' cottage the father is busy with preparing the yarn if he has not gone out to buy yarn or sell the linen that has been produced, or if he does not cultivate the plot of land together with his grown-up son. The mother is occupied about the hearth or tends the animals. The elder daughter sits at the loom and the younger children, still going to school, in their spare time have to wind yarn onto bobbins."

In Germany and elsewhere the benefits of the Industrial Revolution did not fall evenly on all sectors of society.

Cottage industry:
See also
Volume 1 pages 31-33

A German weaver in his run-down workshop in the early 1800s.

LOOKING TOWARD THE FUTURE

MIDCENTURY SUMMARY

The first followers—Belgium, France, Germany—made impressive industrial progress, but they still remained at least a generation behind the leader, Great Britain. The statistics of economic development—railroad mileage, coal and pig iron output, steam power capacity, raw cotton consumption—showed the gap.

Other measures of industrialization further showed Great Britain's unique position. In 1851 about half the people of England and Wales lived in towns, while in France and Germany only one-quarter of the population was urbanized. At midcentury one-quarter of the male British adult work force labored in agriculture. Belgium, the continent's most industrialized country, had half its adult male workers in the farm sector. As late as 1895 more German workers labored in agriculture than industry, while France had more adult males working in the farm sector compared to industry until 1945.

If the continent remained well behind Great Britain in industry and urbanization, it also did not have the ugly factory slums that went hand in hand with British industrialization. Instead, the continent featured a more dispersed, and consequently less visible, rural poverty. Its increasing rural population surpassed the ability of its industry to provide jobs. Consequently ever more people turned to cottage industry and the putting-out system (see Volume 1) to survive. The surplus of cottage workers drove down wages until, in the 1840s, a terrible combination of national economic downturn and famine brought misery and death to many.

By the mid 1800s French cotton mills were equipped with power looms.

PERFECTION BY TRIAL AND ERROR

Until the Industrial Revolution most technical advances came from making small improvements in production methods. The development of industrial processes in such industries as metals, brewing, and dyeing was slow and steady. They came from years of trial and error rather than a knowledge of the science involved. For example, although blast furnaces had been used to separate metal from impurities since the Middle Ages, the chemistry of what took place inside the furnace was not known until the middle of the nineteenth century.

By 1750 the world had only just begun to apply scientific principles to technical problems. The leather-tanning industry is a good example. For as long as anyone could remember, tanners had used tried-and-trusted methods. In the late 1700s the Royal Society encouraged the investigation of tanning methods. The great British scientist Sir Humphry Davy conducted numerous experiments to try to improve tanning. In 1799 he concluded: "...in general, tanners appear to have arrived in consequence of repeated practical experiments, at a degree of perfection which cannot be very far extended" by any known scientific theory.

Tanners had reached a state of perfection independent of any knowledge of science. Likewise, many of the early advances associated with the Industrial Revolution came from men who had little or no formal education. James Brindley, the self-taught genius who built the Duke of Bridgewater's canal, was unable to write. Before embarking on a project, he took to his bed for a few days to think things out, doing all his calculations in his head and without written plan. By this remarkable process Brindley precisely designed and executed over 360 miles of canal work complete with bridges, aqueducts, and underground tunnels.

ECONOMIC DEVELOPMENT				
Railroad mileage (statue miles)	Coal production or consumption (1,000 metric tons)	Pig iron output (1,000 metric tons)	Steam power capacity (1,000 horse power)	Raw cotton consumption (1,000 metric tons)
Great Britain				
1850 6,621	37,500	2,249	1,290	266.1
1869 15,145	97,066	5,446	4,040	425.8
Belgium				
1850 531	3,481	145	70	10.0
1869 1,800	7,822	535	350	16.3
France				
1850 1,869	7,225	406	370	59.3
1869 10,518	21,432	1,381	1,850	93.7
Germany				
1850 3,639	5,100	212	260	17.1
1869 10,834	26,774	1,413	2,480	64.1

Source: *The Cambridge Economic History of Europe*, Vol. VI, pt. 1., p. 423.

The Industrial Revolution showed that there remained room for contributions from men with special talents regardless of lack of education. But times were changing. To an ever increasing extent future invention and innovation would come from men who had received a formal education, and particularly from those who understood science and mathematics. In turn, scientific progress suggested new paths for inventors and tinkerers to explore.

Before the Industrial Revolution most industrial advances came from trial and error. At the start of the nineteenth century it was becoming clear that from now on industrial progress would come from advances in scientific and technological knowledge.

A VISION OF PROGRESS

English leaders recognized that technological progress was valuable for the nation. Private institutions existed that encouraged the sharing of ideas among businessmen, scientists, and inventors. Two great London societies led the way. In 1662 The Royal Society was founded. Its charter stated: "The

The Royal Society meeting at the house that served as its headquarters from 1780 to 1857.

business of the Royal Society is to improve the knowledge of natural things, and all useful arts, Manufactures, Mechanic practices, Engynes [engines] and Inventions by experiment." Its members included the most gifted people in a wide variety of fields, including science and technology. The Royal Society of Arts, founded in 1754, had a similar membership. Its mission was to encourage the "Arts, Manufactures, and Commerce in Great Britain." Its founding members conceived the society to be an active, useful institution to stimulate socially valuable discoveries, inventions, and innovations.

In addition, many regional and local organizations dedicated themselves to the promotion of science. Sometimes members pursued paths that led nowhere or led to wrong conclusions. But the effect of having many groups and organizations engaged in scientific inquiry was important for two main reasons: It promoted the scientific method (observation and experiment), and it slowly developed a better understanding of basic science.

Economic and manufacturing demands required more engineers, particularly those with specialized skills. In the past all engineers were mechanical engineers. Bridge and canal building and harbor design required a different skill set. To meet this need, in 1828 the Institute of Civil Engineers was founded. Its charter explained that the profession of civil engineering was "the art of directing the Great Sources of Power in Nature for the use and convenience of man."

In the past inventors usually jealously guarded their secrets. The development of institutions throughout Europe dedicated to sharing technical and scientific information represented a new vision of progress. Stated in modern terms, these organizations served as information networks. Craftsmen and inventors used the information to help develop the machines that are associated with the Industrial Revolution.

THE TAKEOFF OF THE INDUSTRIAL REVOLUTION

As inventions spread, they provided mutual support for each other. The relationship among coal, steam engines, railroads, and iron dramatically demonstrated this support system at work. Deeper coal mines provided the initial impetus for the development of powerful steam pumps to drain water from the coal seams. A modified steam engine, attached to a frame with wheels, drove railroads. Railroads created enormous demand for mass-produced iron, which relied on coke, which in turn increased demand for coal. Simultaneously, new railways allowed industrialists access to new coal sources.

Industrialization made large contributions to rising productivity, which led to rising incomes. The fact that more people had more money to spend meant that innovators could be reasonably confident that there would be a market for their new products and methods.

Mutually supporting inventions and innovations combined with the growing confidence of innovators to give the world rapid, self-sustaining growth for the first time in history. At the same time, technological change was becoming a familiar aspect of business and industry.

During the ensuing decades revolutionary changes accelerated. Later it could be said that the nineteenth century marked the birth of the modern world.

The Royal Albert Bridge, a railroad bridge in southwestern England, was designed by the great British engineer Isambard Kingdom Brunel and was opened in 1859.

A DATELINE OF MAJOR EVENTS DURING THE INDUSTRIAL REVOLUTION

	BEFORE 1750	1760	1770	1780
REVOLUTIONS IN INDUSTRY AND TECHNOLOGY	**1619:** English settlers establish the first iron works in colonial America, near Jamestown, Virginia. **1689:** Thomas Savery (England) patents the first design for a steam engine. **1709:** Englishman Abraham Darby uses coke instead of coal to fuel his blast furnace. **1712:** Englishman Thomas Newcomen builds the first working steam engine. **1717:** Thomas Lombe establishes a silk-throwing factory in England. **1720:** The first Newcomen steam engine on the Continent is installed at a Belgian coal mine. **1733:** James Kay (England) invents the flying shuttle. **1742:** Benjamin Huntsman begins making crucible steel in England.	**1756:** The first American coal mine opens. **1764:** In England James Hargreaves invents the spinning jenny. **1769:** Englishman Richard Arkwright patents his spinning machine, called a water frame. James Watt of Scotland patents an improved steam engine design. Josiah Wedgwood (England) opens his Etruria pottery works.	**1771:** An industrial spy smuggles drawings of the spinning jenny from England to France. **1774:** John Wilkinson (England) builds machines for boring cannon cylinders. **1775:** Arkwright patents carding, drawing, and roving machines. In an attempt to end dependence on British textiles American revolutionaries open a spinning mill in Philadelphia using a smuggled spinning-jenny design. **1777:** Oliver Evans (U.S.) invents a card-making machine. **1778:** John Smeaton (England) introduces cast iron gearing to transfer power from waterwheels to machinery. The water closet (indoor toilet) is invented in England. **1779:** Englishman Samuel Crompton develops the spinning mule.	**1783:** Englishman Thomas Bell invents a copper cylinder to print patterns on fabrics. **1784:** Englishman Henry Cort invents improved rollers for rolling mills and the puddling process for refining pig iron. Frenchman Claude Berthollet discovers that chlorine can be used as a bleach. The ironworks at Le Creusot use France's first rotary steam engine to power its hammers, as well as using the Continent's first coke-fired blast furnace. **1785:** Englishman Edmund Cartwright invents the power loom. **1788:** The first steam engine is imported into Germany.
REVOLUTIONS IN TRANSPORTATION AND COMMUNICATION		**1757:** The first canal is built in England. Locks on an English canal		**1785:** The first canal is built in the United States, at Richmond, Virginia. **1787:** John Fitch and James Rumsey (U.S.) each succeed in launching a working steamboat.
SOCIAL REVOLUTIONS	**1723:** Britain passes an act to allow the establishment of workhouses for the poor.	**1750:** The enclosure of common land gains momentum in Britain.	**1776:** Scottish professor Adam Smith publishes *The Wealth of Nations*, which promotes laissez-faire capitalism.	The workhouse
INTERNATIONAL RELATIONS	Continental Army in winter quarters at Valley Forge		**1775–1783:** The American Revolution. Thirteen colonies win their independence from Great Britain and form a new nation, the United States of America.	**1789–1793:** The French Revolution leads to abolition of the monarchy and execution of the king and queen. Mass executions follow during the Reign of Terror, 1793–1794.

1790	1800	1810	1820

1790: English textile producer Samuel Slater begins setting up America's first successful textile factory in Pawtucket, Rhode Island.

Jacob Perkins (U.S.) invents a machine capable of mass-producing nails.

1791: French chemist Nicholas Leblanc invents a soda-making process.

1793: Eli Whitney (U.S.) invents a cotton gin.

1794: Germany's first coke-fired blast furnace is built.

The first German cotton spinning mill installs Arkwright's water frame.

1798: Eli Whitney devises a system for using power-driven machinery to produce interchangeable parts, the model for the "American System" of manufacture.

Wool-spinning mills are built in Belgium using machinery smuggled out of England.

A cylindrical papermaking machine is invented in England.

1801: American inventor Oliver Evans builds the first working high-pressure steam engine and uses it to power a mill.

Joseph-Marie Jacquard (France) invents a loom that uses punch cards to produce patterned fabrics.

A cotton-spinning factory based on British machinery opens in Belgium.

The first cotton-spinning mill in Switzerland begins operation.

Austria establishes the Continent's largest cotton-spinning mill.

1802: In England William Murdock uses coal gas to light an entire factory.

Richard Trevithick builds a high-pressure steam engine in England.

1807: British businessmen open an industrial complex in Belgium that includes machine manufacture, coal mining, and iron production.

1808: Russia's first spinning mill begins production in Moscow.

1810: Henry Maudslay (England) invents the precision lathe.

1816: Steam power is used for the first time in an American paper mill.

English scientist Humphry Davy invents a safety lamp for coal miners in England.

1817: The French iron industry's first puddling works and rolling mills are established.

1819: Thomas Blanchard (U.S.) invents a gunstock-turning lathe, which permits production of standardized parts.

A turning lathe

1821: Massachusetts businessmen begin developing Lowell as a site for textile mills.

1822: Power looms are introduced in French factories.

1820s: Spinning mills begin operation in Sweden.

Steam power is first used in Czech industry.

1827: A water-driven turbine is invented in France.

1794: The 66-mile Philadelphia and Lancaster turnpike begins operation.

Along an American Highway

1802: In England Richard Trevithick builds his first steam locomotive.

1807: Robert Fulton launches the Clermont, the first commercially successful steamboat, on the Hudson River in New York.

1811: Robert Fulton and his partner launch the first steamboat on the Mississippi River.

Construction begins on the Cumberland Road (later renamed the National Road) from Baltimore, Maryland, to Wheeling, Virginia.

1815: In England John McAdam develops an improved technique for surfacing roads.

1819: The first steamship crosses the Atlantic Ocean.

1825: The 363-mile Erie Canal is completed in America.

In England the first passenger railroad, the Stockton and Darlington Railway, begins operation.

1826: The 2-mile horse-drawn Granite Railroad in Massachusetts becomes the first American railroad.

1790: First American patent law passed.

Philadelphia begins building a public water system.

1798: Robert Owen takes over the New Lanark mills and begins implementing his progressive ideas.

1800: Parliament prohibits most labor union activity.

1802: Parliament passes a law limiting the working hours of poor children and orphans.

1811–1816: Luddite rioters destroy textile machinery in England.

1819: Parliament extends legal protection to all child laborers.

British cavalry fire at demonstrators demanding voting reform in Manchester, killing 11 and wounding hundreds, including women and children.

1827: Carpenters organize the first national trade union in Britain.

18th–century carpenter

1799: Napoleon Bonaparte seizes control of France's government.

1792–1815: The Napoleonic Wars involve most of Europe, Great Britain, and Russia. France occupies many of its neighboring nations, reorganizes their governments, and changes their borders.

1812–1815: War between the United States and Great Britain disrupts America's foreign trade and spurs the development of American industry.

A DATELINE OF MAJOR EVENTS DURING THE INDUSTRIAL REVOLUTION

	1830	1840	1850	1860
REVOLUTIONS IN INDUSTRY AND TECHNOLOGY	1830: Switzerland's first weaving mill established. 1831: British researcher Michael Faraday builds an electric generator. American inventor Cyrus McCormick builds a horse-drawn mechanical reaper. 1834: Bulgaria's first textile factory is built. 1835: Samuel Colt (U.S)invents the Colt revolver. The first steam engine is used to power a paper mill in Croatia. 1836: The first Hungarian steam mill, the Pest Rolling Mill company, begins using steam power to process grain. 1837: The first successful coke-fired blast furnace in the United States begins operation.	American blacksmith John Deere introduces the first steel plow. 1842: Britain lifts restrictions on exporting textile machinery. Making Bessemer steel	1849: The California Gold Rush begins. 1850: Swedish sawmills begin using steam power. 1851: The Great Exhibition opens at the Crystal Palace in London. William Kelly of Kentucky invents a process for converting pig iron to steel. 1852: Hydraulic mining is introduced in the American West. 1853: The first cotton-spinning mill opens in India. 1856: William Perkin (England) synthesizes the first coal tar dye. Henry Bessemer (England) announces his process for converting pig iron to steel. Isaac Singer (U.S.) introduces the sewing machine.	1859: Edwin Drake successfully drills for oil in Pennsylvania. 1863: Ernest Solvay of Belgium begins working on a process to recover ammonia from soda ash in order to produce bleaching powder. 1864: Switzerland's first major chemical company is established. The Siemens-Martin open-hearth steelmaking process is perfected in France. 1865: The first oil pipeline opens in America. The rotary web press is invented in America, permitting printing on both sides of the paper. 1866: U.S. government surveyors discover the largest-known deposit of iron ore in the world in the Mesabi Range of northern Minnesota.
REVOLUTIONS IN TRANSPORTATION AND COMMUNICATION	1830: The first locomotive-powered railroad to offer regular service begins operating in South Carolina. The opening of the Liverpool and Manchester Railway marks the beginning of the British railroad boom. 1833: The 60-mile Camden and Amboy Railroad of New Jersey is completed. 1835: Construction begins on Germany's first railroad.	1836: First railroad built in Russia. 1843: Tunnel completed under the Thames River, London, England, the world's first to be bored through soft clay under a riverbed. 1844: Samuel Morse (U.S.) sends the first message via his invention, the telegraph. The nation's first steam-powered sawmill begins operation on the West Coast.	1846: First railroad built in Hungary. 1853: The first railway is completed in India. 1854: Americans complete the Moscow-St. Petersburg railroad line. 1855: Switzerland's first railroad opens.	1859: In France Etienne Lenoir invents an internal combustion engine. 1860–1861: The Pony Express, a system of relay riders, carries mail to and from America's West Coast. 1866: The transatlantic telegraph cable is completed. Congress authorizes construction of a transcontinental telegraph line. 1869: The tracks of two railroad companies meet at Promontory, Utah, to complete America's first transcontinental railroad
SOCIAL REVOLUTIONS	1833: Parliament passes the Factory Act to protect children working in textile factories. 1836–1842: The English Chartist movement demands Parliamentary reform, but its petitions are rejected by Parliament. 1838: The U.S. Congress passes a law regulating steamboat boiler safety, the first attempt by the federal government to regulate private behavior in the interest of public safety.	1842: Parliament bans the employment of children and women underground in mines. 1845: Russia bans strikes. 1847: A new British Factory Act limits working hours to 10 hours a day or 58 hours a week for children aged 13 to 18 and for women. 1848: Marx and Engels coauthor the Communist Manifesto.	1854: In England Charles Dickens publishes *Hard Times*, a novel based on his childhood as a factory worker. 1857: Brooklyn, New York, builds a city wastewater system.	1860–1910: More than 20 million Europeans emigrate to the United States. 1866: National Labor Union forms in the United States. 1869: Knights of Labor forms in the United States. Founding of the Great Atlantic and Pacific Tea Company (A&P) in the U.S.
INTERNATIONAL RELATIONS	1839–1842: Great Britain defeats China in a war and forces it to open several ports to trade.	1847: Austro-Hungary occupies Italy. 1848: Failed revolutions take place in France, Germany, and Austro-Hungary. Serfdom ends in Austro-Hungary.	1853: The American naval officer Commodore Matthew Perry arrives in Japan. 1853–1856: France, Britain, and Turkey defeat Russia in the Crimean War. 1858: Great Britain takes control of India, retaining it until 1947.	1861–1865: The American Civil War brings about the end of slavery in the United States and disrupts raw cotton supplies for U.S. and foreign cotton mills. 1867: Britain gains control of parts of Malaysia. Malaysia is a British colony from 1890 to 1957.

1870	1880	1890	1900

1860s: Agricultural machinery introduced in Hungary.

1870: John D. Rockefeller establishes the Standard Oil Company (U.S.).

1873: The Bethlehem Steel Company begins operation in Pennsylvania.

1875: The first modern iron and steel works opens in India.

Investment in the Japan's cotton industry booms.

1876: Philadelphia hosts the Centennial Exposition.

1877: Hungary installs its first electrical system.

1879: Charles Brush builds the nation's first arc-lighting system in San Francisco.

Thomas Edison (U.S.) develops the first practical incandescent light bulb.

1870s: Japan introduces mechanical silk-reeling.

1882: In New York City the Edison Electric Illuminating Company begins operating the world's first centralized electrical generating station.

1884: The U.S. Circuit Court bans hydraulic mining.

George Westinghouse (U.S.) founds Westinghouse Electric Company.

English engineer Charles Parsons develops a steam turbine.

1885: The introduction of band saws makes American lumbering more efficient.

German inventor Carl Benz builds a self-propelled vehicle powered by a single cylinder gas engine with electric ignition.

1887: An English power plant is the first to use steam turbines to generate electricity.

1888: Nikola Tesla (U.S.) invents an

alternating current electric motor.

1894: An American cotton mill becomes the first factory ever built to rely entirely on electric power.

1895: George Westinghouse builds the world's first generating plant designed to transmit power over longer distances—a hydroelectric plant at Niagara Falls to

transmit alternating current some 20 miles to consumers in Buffalo, New York.

1901: The United States Steel Corporation is formed by a merger of several American companies.

Japan opens its first major iron and steel works.

1929: The U.S.S.R. begins implementing its first Five-Year Plan, which places nationwide industrial development under central government control.

Power generators at Edison Electric

1875: Japan builds its first railway.

1876: In the U.S. Alexander Graham Bell invents the telephone.

German inventor Nikolaus Otto produces a practical gasoline engine.

1870s: Sweden's railroad boom.

1883: Brooklyn Bridge completed.

1885: Germans Gottlieb Daimler and Wilhelm Maybach build the world's first motorcycle.

1886: Daimler and Maybach invent the carburetor, the device that efficiently mixes fuel and air in internal combustion engines

1888: The first electric urban streetcar system begins operation in Richmond, Virginia.

1893: American brothers Charles and J. Frank Duryea build a working gasoline-powered automobile.

1896: Henry Ford builds a demonstration car powered by an internal combustion engine.

1896–1904: Russia builds the Manchurian railway in China.

1903: Henry Ford establishes Ford Motor Company.

1904: New York City subway system opens.

Trans-Siberian Railroad completed.

1908: William Durant, maker of horse-drawn carriages, forms the General Motors Company.

1909: Ford introduces the Model T automobile.

1870: Parliament passes a law to provide free schooling for poor children.

1872: France bans the International Working Men's Association.

1874: France applies its child labor laws to all industrial establishments and provides for inspectors to enforce the laws.

1877: Wage cuts set off the Great Railroad Strike in West Virginia, and the strike spreads across the country. Federal troops kill 35 strikers.

1880: Parliament makes school attendance compulsory for children between the ages of 5 and 10.

1881: India passes a factory law limiting child employment.

1884: Germany passes a law requiring employers to provide insurance against workplace accidents.

1886: American Federation of Labor forms.

1887: U.S. Interstate Commerce Act passed to regulate railroad freight charges.

1890: The U.S. government outlaws monopolies with passage of the Sherman Antitrust Act.

1892: Workers strike at Carnegie Steel in Homestead, Pennsylvania, in response to wage cuts. An armed confrontation results in 12 deaths.

1894: The Pullman strike, called in response to wage cuts, halts American railroad traffic. A confrontation with 2,000 federal troops kills 12 strikers in Chicago.

1900: Japan passes a law to limit union activity.

1902: The United Mine Workers calls a nationwide strike against coal mines, demanding eight-hour workdays and higher wages.

1903: Socialists organize the Russian Social Democratic Workers Party.

1931: Japan passes a law to limit working hours for women and children in textile factories.

1870: The city-states of Italy unify to form one nation.

1871: Parisians declare self-government in the city but are defeated by government forces.

Prussia and the other German states unify to form the German Empire.

1877–1878: War between Russia and Turkey. Bulgaria gains independence from Turkey.

1900–1901: A popular uprising supported by the Chinese government seeks to eject all foreigners from China.

1917: Russian Revolution

1929: A worldwide economic depression begins.

REVOLUTIONARY THINKERS

CHARLES BABBAGE: 1792–1871; born in England. A mathematician and professor at Cambridge University, Babbage built a model of a calculator that could add large numbers. He then designed what he called an "analytical engine" that would use machine-readable punchcards—derived from the Jacquard loom—to perform calculations. His design, now considered the forerunner of modern computer technology, was never built because nobody at that time could make sufficiently precise metal parts. It lay forgotten until 1937, when his notes were found. Babbage also invented an opthalmoscope for viewing the inside of the eye and the "cowcatcher" for locomotives.

JAMES BRINDLEY: 1716–1772; born in England. The uneducated son of a farm laborer, Brindley started out as an apprentice millwright and became a brilliant and successful civil engineer. He built more than 300 miles of canals and designed locks, tunnels, and barges for them. Brindley built Great Britain's first raised aqueduct to carry a canal across a river. He designed all of his projects entirely in his head and left no drawings or written records.

ISAMBARD KINGDOM BRUNEL: 1806–1859; born in England. Considered Great Britain's most brilliant railroad engineer, Brunel designed stations, tunnels, and bridges, including the Royal Albert Bridge. Brunel built more than 1,000 miles of track in the British Isles as well as railways in Europe and India. He also built a steamboat with a screw propeller and a trans-Atlantic steamer that made more than 60 crossings to and from New York. Among his many innovative projects was a prefabricated field hospital building that was shipped in pieces to a war zone in Russia (Crimean War, 1853–1856) and reassembled on site.

MARC ISAMBARD BRUNEL: 1769–1849; born in France. Marc Brunel served in the French navy. During the French Revolution he supported the royalists and was forced to flee the country. He settled in the United States and worked as New York City's chief engineer. He moved to England in 1799. Father of Isambard Kingdom Brunel, the elder Brunel designed buildings, engines, and machinery, including pulley-block-making machines. A series of business failures sent him to debtors prison in 1821, and his friends raised the funds for his release. Marc Brunel also developed the tunneling shield, which made possible the building of a tunnel under the Thames River, the world's first tunnel to be bored into the ground underneath a river.

WILLIAM COCKERILL: 1759–1832; born in England. Cockerill was a skilled mechanic who built models of machines. He took on work assignments in Russia and Sweden. At the age of 40 he moved to a part of France that later became part of Belgium and built Europe's first wool-carding and spinning machines. Within a few years Cockerill and his sons had opened their own factory to make spinning machines and mechanical looms.

HUMPHRY DAVY: 1778–1829; born in England. Apprenticed to a surgeon, Davy wrote poetry in his spare time. He eventually abandoned poetry as he became fascinated by his study of chemistry. Davy discovered several of the chemical elements, including sodium and potassium, invented the safety lamp for miners, and became well known for his scientific lectures. He built a battery-operated electric arc lamp but was so far ahead of his time that no practical use could be found for it.

BENOIT FOURNEYRON: 1802–1867; born in France. Fourneyron attended engineering school and then worked at the Le Creusot iron works. While at Le Creusot, he developed a small water-powered turbine. Within a few years he built a turbine capable of making 2,300 revolutions per minute. Numerous European factories installed Fourneyron's turbines, as did American textile mills. Many years after his death Fourneyron's turbine powered an American electrical generation plant at Niagara Falls.

JOSEPH-MARIE JACQUARD: 1752–1834; born in France. Jacquard originated the use of punchcards on drawlooms. The cards automated the production of patterned fabrics and were later applied by others to the operation of computing machines. (See page 50 of this volume for more about Jacquard.)

PHILIPPE LEBON: 1767–1804; born in France. Lebon was a chemist, a professor of engineering, and a working engineer. He invented gas lighting based on wood gas. He is also believed to have designed a gasoline engine. Lebon met a mysterious end while working to prepare for Napoleon's coronation as emperor. He may have been murdered by intruders on the day of the coronation.

HENRY MAUDSLAY: 1771–1831; born in England. The inventor and maker of precision nuts, bolts, and machine tools also built steam engines for ships. (See page 6 of this volume for more about Maudslay.)

WILLIAM MURDOCK: 1754–1839; born in Scotland. Murdock built engines for a living and turned his talents to invention. He invented coal-gas lighting, which was used for both interior and street lighting, but he never patented the invention. He also made a number of improvements to Watt's steam engine. Murdock managed a major engine parts factory for more than 30 years.

JEAN-VICTOR PONCELET: 1788–1867; born in France. A mathematician and engineer, Poncelet served under Napoleon in Russia and was wounded and imprisoned. As a prisoner of war, he originated some of the concepts of modern geometry. After his release and return to France he continued his work as a military engineer and a professor. He successfully applied his mathematical concepts to the task of designing more efficient turbines.

JOHN SMEATON: 1724–1792; born in England. Smeaton, a maker of mathematical instruments, founded Great Britain's Society of Civil Engineers. After touring Europe and studying its canals and harbors, he designed and built a lighthouse whose dovetailed stone block construction withstood the elements on a site where two previous lighthouses had been destroyed. He also worked on canals, bridges, harbors, and a diving bell, in addition to making improvements to the waterwheel.

GEORGE STEPHENSON: 1781–1848; born in England. Stephenson was born in a one-room cottage and did not attend school. He began his working life as an engine operator and mechanic. As an adult Stephenson attended night school to learn how to read and write. He made sure his son received an education and studied his son's homework in order to learn more. He earned additional money by repairing shoes and clocks, and went on to build the first practical locomotive and design entire railways.

RICHARD TREVITHICK: 1771–1833; born in England. Trevithick did poorly in school, and his teacher described him as disobedient and slow. Despite his lack of education, he possessed an intuitive talent for solving engineering problems. Trevithick developed a high-pressure steam engine designed to sidestep James Watt's patented engine. Trevithick applied his engine to mining, pumping, agricultural machinery, and a steam carriage for passengers. He went to Peru to set up engines to pump out silver mines. In spite of his skill, his various ventures failed, and he died in poverty.

JAMES WATT: 1736–1819; born in Scotland. As a child, Watt spent long hours in his father's workshop building models. At the age of 17 he sought out training as a maker of mathematical instruments (such as scales) and several years later began working at the university in Glasgow. There Watt improved Newcomen's steam engine and produced a more efficient and powerful model that saw wide use. He interrupted his experiments with the steam engine to work as a land surveyor mapping out routes for canals. Unlike many inventors, Watt achieved wealth and recognition during his lifetime. (See Volume 2 for more about Watt.)

GLOSSARY

ARISTOCRAT: a person born into the upper class of society

BARGE: a flat-bottomed boat, usually used on inland waterways

BLAST FURNACE: a tall furnace that uses a blast of air to generate intense heat capable of melting iron and processing it into a purer form

BLOCK AND TACKLE: pulleys (blocks) and ropes (tackle) used to raise and lower heavy objects such as sails

BREAST WHEEL: waterwheel turned by water dropping onto it midway between the top and bottom of the wheel

CAPITAL: money or property used in operating a business

CAPITALIST: a person who invests money in a business

CHARCOAL: a fuel made by charring wood in a buried fire so that very little air enters the fire

CIVIL ENGINEER: engineer who specializes in the design and construction of public works such as bridges, roads, canals, and waterworks

COAL GAS: gas produced by burning coal, used as a fuel for lighting

COKE: a form of coal that has been heated to remove gases so that it burns with great heat and little smoke

COMPOUND ENGINE: a steam engine that gets more work out of the steam by compressing it and allowing it to expand multiple times

CONTINENTAL: European; pertaining to the continent of Europe. The islands that make up Great Britain are not considered part of the continent.

COTTAGE INDUSTRY: manufacturing goods at home

CUSTOMS: the authority that regulates and collects taxes on imports and exports

CYLINDER: the round chamber in an engine where steam expands and contracts to move a piston

DRAWLOOM: a loom for the weaving of patterned cloth

FORGE: a site where iron is heated in a fire and shaped by hammering

IRONMASTER: one who manufactures iron

JACQUARD: the type of patterned cloth woven on a Jacquard loom

JIG: a pattern piece, usually of metal, used as a guide for shaping and duplicating an object with a power tool

LATHE: a machine for shaping pieces of wood or metal that works by rapidly turning the piece to be shaped against a stationary cutting edge

LOCOMOTIVE: railroad car containing an engine and used to pull a train

LUDDITES: name given to English artisans who destroyed the new textile machinery that they feared would replace them; their imaginary leader was Ned Ludd

MACADAM: type of stone road surface named after its inventor, John McAdam

MACHINE TOOLS: tools used to make machines or parts of machines

METALLURGY: the science of extracting metals from ores and refining them for use

METHANE: an odorless, easy to ignite gas that occurs naturally in coal mines and oil wells

OVERSHOT WATERWHEEL: waterwheel turned by water falling onto the top of the wheel

PARLIAMENT: the legislature of Great Britain, consisting of an upper house called the House of Lords and a lower house called the House of Commons

PATENT: legal document granting the exclusive right to produce and profit from an invention; the act of obtaining a patent

PIG IRON: the product created by smelting iron ore in a furnace

PISTON: a disk or short rod made to closely fit in an engine cylinder so that changes in pressure inside the cylinder cause the piston to move. The motion of the piston is then used to drive machinery, such as the paddle wheel of a steamboat or the wheels of a locomotive.

PUDDLING: a process for converting pig iron to wrought iron by melting and stirring it

PUTTING-OUT SYSTEM: sending out work, such as spinning or weaving, to be done by workers at home

STEAM ENGINE: an engine that uses steam under pressure to produce power. In the most basic form of steam engine steam enters a cylinder and is then compressed with a piston.

TANNING: using tannic acid (derived from oak bark) to process animal hides into leather

TECHNOLOGY TRANSFER: the movement of modern technologies from one place to another

TURBINE: a wheel-shaped engine driven by steam or water pressure on its curved spokes

TURNPIKE: toll road blocked by a pike, or tollgate, where tolls are collected

UNDERSHOT WATERWHEEL: waterwheel placed directly in a stream so that it is turned by the water flowing under it

VOLATILE: rapidly evaporating and easy to ignite

ADDITIONAL RESOURCES

BOOKS:

Bland, Celia. *The Mechanical Age: The Industrial Revolution in England.* New York: Facts on File, 1995.

Bridgman, Roger. *Inventions and Discoveries.* London: Dorling-Kindersley Publishing, 2002.

Gies, Frances and Joseph. *Cathedral, Forge, and Waterwheel: Technology and Invention in the Middle Ages.* New York: Harper Collins, 1994.

Ingpen, Robert, Robert R. Wilkinson, and Philip Wilkinson. *Encyclopedia of Ideas That Changed the World.* New York: Viking, 1993.

Lines, Clifford. *Companion to the Industrial Revolution.* New York: Facts on File, 1990

Macaulay, David. *Mill.* Boston: Houghton Mifflin Co., 1983.

Macaulay, David. *The Way Things Work.* Boston: Houghton Mifflin Co., 1988.

WEBSITES:

http:/www.bbc.co.uk/history/
Links to timelines and activities on a wide range of topics, such as the development of the steam engine

http://www.fordham.edu/halsall/
Select Modern History Sourcebook, then Industrial Revolution – provides links to excerpts from historical texts

http://www.ironbridge.org.uk/discover.asp
Virtual tour of Ironbridge Gorge, site of an ironworks considered the birthplace of the Industrial Revolution in England

http://www.drcm.org.uk/default.htm
Website of the Darlington Railway Museum

SET INDEX

Bold numbers refer to volumes